Ch 3-96   15.60

# basketball

# the
## SUMMER OLYMPICS

# basketball

## SUMMER OLYMPICS

PUBLISHED BY SMART APPLE MEDIA

Published by Smart Apple Media
123 South Broad Street, Mankato, Minnesota 56001

Cover Illustration by Eric Melhorn

Designed by Core Design

Photos by: Allsport, Bettmann Archives, Library of Congress and Wide World Photos

Copyright © 1995 Smart Apple Media.
International copyrights reserved in all countries.
No part of this book may be reproduced in any form without written permission from the publisher.
Printed in the United States of America.

**Library of Congress Cataloging-in-Publication Data**

DiMeglio, John E.
Basketball / by John DiMcglio.
(The Summer Olympics)
Includes index.
Summary: Traces the history of basketball as an Olympic sport.

**ISBN 1-887068-06-6**

1. Basketball—Juvenile literature. 2. Olympics—Juvenile literature. [1. Basketball—History. 2. Olympics.] I. Title. II. Series.

GV885.1.D55 1995          95-11968
796.323—dc20

## FROM PEACH BASKETS TO THE OLYMPICS

In December 1891, the International YMCA Training School in Springfield, Massachusetts, brought its gym classes indoors in cold weather. One class tired of its routine and grew unruly. James Naismith, a young Canadian-born teacher, took over and created a new game: Peach baskets were nailed to balconies at each end of the gym, and players passed the ball back

*Basketball has come a long way since 1891.*

Dr. James Naismith, "Father of Basketball."

and forth until one team scored by throwing the ball into a basket. Basketball was born.

The game caught on quickly as the school's graduates took jobs in YMCAs all over the United States and Canada and brought the game with them. Today basketball is one of the most popular sports in the world, ranging from pickup games in parks to thrilling professional championships. It's not surprising, then, that basketball has long been celebrated in Olympic competition.

As the 1996 Atlanta Summer Games draw closer, sports fans around the globe will be expecting another gold medal for the United States. Dream Team I—consisting mostly of National Basketball Association (NBA) superstars such as Charles Barkley, Larry Bird, Michael Jordan and Earvin "Magic" Johnson—made a shambles of the 1992 competition in Barcelona, Spain. In Atlanta, Dream Team II will be out to prove it is just as good.

Along the way, basketball fans are sure to be treated to amazing displays of athletic skill that can't be found in any other sport.

## **BECOMING OFFICIAL**

Basketball first appeared in the Olympic Games in St. Louis in 1904. It was played as a demonstration sport, without official medals. A Buffalo, New York, team won easily against

*Basketball is a game of power and grace (pages 10-11).*

a small field in an Olympics attended by very few countries.

In 1924 in Paris, and 1928 in Amsterdam, basketball was again played as an Olympic demonstration sport. Then, in the 1932 Los Angeles Games, it was dropped in favor of lacrosse and college football. Angered by this, leaders of basketball programs formed a world association and asked for entry into the next Olympics. Their request was granted, and at the 1936 Olympic Games in Berlin, basketball was official for the first time.

*The first official Olympic basketball competition was held in 1936.*

Twenty-one nations sent teams. Canada and the United States played for the gold as Naismith, the man who had invented the game, looked on. His indoor game was played outdoors on clay and sand tennis courts because Berlin lacked appropriate indoor arenas. Pouring rain ruined the surface, but the United States managed a messy 19-8 win.

## THE AMERICANS RULE

World War II canceled the Olympics in 1940 and 1944, so the Americans weren't able to defend their championship until the 1948 Games in London. By this time, basketball was played in over 75 countries, 23 of which sent teams to London.

New developments in the game were taking place. Dribbling was a more important part of the game, and one-handed shots were replacing standard two-handed shots. The Americans adapted better to these new developments, so while the United States moved ahead, other countries lagged behind.

Would others close the gap? Through several Olympiads it appeared none could. U.S. teams kept winning, usually by lopsided scores. They humbled opponents. If they weren't trouncing Switzerland 86-21 in 1948, they were walloping Chile 103-55 in 1952. In 1956 Bill Russell delayed signing with the Boston Celtics to play in Melbourne, and the U.S. ran away with scores like 101-29 (against Thailand) and 121-53 (against the Philippines). Their closest game was 89-55 against the Soviets in the final.

In 1960 in Rome, many said the Americans had their best team yet. Oscar Robertson, Jerry West and Jerry Lucas—future NBA stars—headed an outstanding roster. The United States breezed to a gold medal, first mangling future powerhouse Yugoslavia 104-42, then easily defeating Brazil 90-63.

*The modern game stresses finesse in ball-handling.*

## CLOSING THE GAP

Although the United States stayed on top of the opposition, some nations were coming closer. One reason was the system of forming Olympic teams. Americans organized just weeks before the competition. Many others sent squads that had played together for years. These veterans knew each other better, an obvious benefit on the court.

Furthermore, such American basketball experts as Red Auerbach and Bob Cousy conducted clinics around the world in the 1950s and 1960s. Global basketball improved greatly because of their efforts, and Olympic basketball scores became less lopsided. In Tokyo in 1964, the United States won the gold against the Soviets, 73-59. Bill Bradley captained and Luke Jackson led the scoring in the final.

In Mexico City four years later it appeared, finally, the U.S. team might lose. Its two best amateurs were absent. Lew Alcindor (later known as Kareem Abdul-Jabbar) refused to interrupt his college studies, adding that he sympathized with a possible Olympic boycott by African-Americans. Elvin Hayes signed a pro contract, making him ineligible.

Facing Yugoslavia for the gold, the Americans faltered—until Spencer Haywood and Jo-Jo White got hot. The United States won 65-50 for another gold.

## CONTROVERSY AND A COMEBACK

Then, it happened. America's winning streak, which started in Berlin in 1936, ended in another German city, Munich, in 1972.

Entering the final against the Soviet Union, the Americans had won 62 Olympic games in a row. Coach Hank Iba again headed a talented but inexperienced squad. The Soviets, on the

*Competition between U.S. and Soviet teams has always been intense.*

other hand, were veterans of international play and led from the start.

Three seconds remained when free throws by Doug Collins put the United States ahead, 50-49. It was their first lead. Total chaos followed. The Soviet Union inbounded, but play was halted when a referee called for an administrative time-out. After considerable confusion, the clock was set back to three seconds. This time a court-length pass to Aleksandr Belov resulted in a buzzer-beating basket. The American team had finally lost.

The referee refused to sign the scorebook. Official U.S. protests were denied, and the Americans were so frustrated that they refused their silver medals.

Winning back the gold was the mission for coach Dean Smith in 1976, America's bicentennial. But the anticipated rematch between the Soviet Union and the United States never happened. Yugoslavia upset the Soviets in the semifinals, 89-84, then lost to the United States, 95-74. America once again had the gold.

The 1976 Games in Montreal were important for another reason as well: Women's basketball finally became an Olympic sport. The U.S. squad included Lusia Harris, Ann Meyers, and 16-year-old Nancy Lieberman. However, they couldn't match the Soviet Union. The Soviets had not lost in international competition in five years. They were led by Iuliyana Semenova, who was nearly 7 feet tall (2.13 m) and weighed 284 pounds (129 kg). Playing less than half the time, she averaged 19.4 points and 12.4

rebounds per game. The Soviets garnered the gold, while the United States settled for the silver.

### FROM MOSCOW TO SEOUL

The United States and the Soviet Union were psyched for 1980 in Moscow. The American women trained vigorously in hopes of winning their first gold. The Soviet men wanted to prove that their 1972 championship was deserved. But politics inter-

*Women's basketball has met the Olympic challenge since 1976.*

fered. Responding to the Soviet invasion of Afghanistan in late 1979, President Jimmy Carter announced a boycott of the Moscow Olympics. American athletes stayed home.

In Moscow, the Soviet women trampled their opponents. Iuliyana Semenova keyed the gold-medal victory over Bulgaria, 104-73.

In men's play, with the home-team Soviets expected to win, a shocker resulted. Yugoslavia won the gold—against Italy! The Soviet Union finished third.

The next Olympic Games were held in Los Angeles in 1984, and this time the Soviet Union boycotted the competition. The long-awaited Soviet and American men's and women's rematches were again postponed.

A powerful U.S. men's team starred Michael Jordan and Patrick Ewing and was coached by Bobby Knight. Aided by outstanding play from Leon Wood and Alvin Robertson, the United States tore through the field, stuffing Spain in the final, 96-65.

The U.S. women followed suit. Cheryl Miller, Anne Donovan and Lynette Woodard, coached by Pat Head-Summitt, who had played in the 1976 Olympics, scorched Korea 85-55 for the gold.

At Seoul in 1988, with no boycotts, the U.S. women proved they could hold their own against a full international field. They defended their gold by defeating Yugoslavia 77-70.

*Going for the gold with grace and style (page 23).*

*International play highlights exciting action under the net.*

In men's competition, the Soviet Union battered Yugoslavia for the championship, 76-63. The American team, coached by John Thompson, was headed by David Robinson and Danny Manning. Getting only the bronze aggravated America's basketball establishment.

## THE DREAM TEAM

Following the 1988 Olympics, the cry went up to allow NBA players—America's best—to represent the United States. In 1989, eligibility rules were changed by the International Basketball Federation. Open competition was permitted, which meant that NBA players were finally able to compete in the Olympics. When the 1992 American roster was named, Michael Jordan, Magic Johnson, Larry Bird and Charles Barkley drew the greatest attention. Christian Laettner was the only collegian. NBA coach Chuck Daly was in charge.

Also affecting Olympic basketball was the fact that the Soviet Union and Yugoslavia no longer existed. America's two strongest basketball rivals had divided into several nations with different teams. Croatia, once a part of Yugoslavia, won the silver, while Lithuania, formerly a Soviet republic, took the bronze.

The Americans dominated in Barcelona. Labeled the "Dream Team," they made each game a romp and showed that they were the best anywhere. Even players on other teams sought the Americans' autographs and asked them to pose for photos.

*Often the action rises above the rim (pages 26-27).*

The closest encounter for the Dream Team was the final against Toni Kukoc and Croatia, 117-85. The win raised America's Olympic record to 93-2 and 10 gold medals in a dozen tries.

In women's play, former Soviet Union players joined together to form the Unified Team, which would prove to be a roadblock for the U.S. team. The American women had demolished Czechoslovakia 111-55 in their opener, setting an American Olympic scoring record. After drilling China 93-67, they set a new record against host Spain, 114-59. However, the United States went cold against the Unified Team. A slowed-down tempo stifled the Americans in a seesaw game and the former Soviets won, 79-73. The Unified Team went on to defeat China 76-66, while the American women defeated Cuba 88-74, adding a bronze medal to their two golds and one silver.

## A LOOK AHEAD

The future holds many exciting possibilities for Olympic basketball. Women's basketball is sure to improve in the years to come. It must be remembered that women have been playing full-court basketball, as contrasted to a divided-court game, only since 1971. They've had national collegiate tournaments only since 1969. As women's sports receive greater emphasis in high schools and colleges, skill levels will rise and women's basketball in the Olympics will benefit.

In men's basketball, it's almost certain that American NBA players will continue to reign. However, the future will bring stiffer competition. Professional leagues are thriving elsewhere, especially in Europe. Satellite television brings to other nations the best basketball America offers, stimulating their interest. International players dot NBA and collegiate rosters.

From a game invented in a gym class, using peach baskets and a soccer ball, basketball has become one of the most exciting of all sports. In 1996, America's Dream Team II will provide plenty of thrills as the team attempts to defend the gold against the world's best. Courtside in Atlanta will be a hot ticket!

*The Dream Team brought international competition to new heights.*

# SUMMER GAMES CHAMPIONS:

# basketball

### Men's Competition

| Year | Final Game Score |
|---|---|
| 1936 | United States 19, Canada 8 |
| 1940 | * |
| 1944 | * |
| 1948 | United States 65, France 21 |
| 1952 | United States 36, USSR 25 |
| 1956 | United States 89, USSR 55 |
| 1960 | United States 90, Brazil 63 |
| 1964 | United States 73, USSR 59 |
| 1968 | United States 65, Yugoslavia 50 |
| 1972 | USSR 51, United States 50 |
| 1976 | United States 95, Yugoslavia 74 |
| 1980 | Yugoslavia 86, Italy 77 |
| 1984 | United States 96, Spain 65 |
| 1988 | USSR 76, Yugoslavia 63 |
| 1992 | United States 117, Croatia 85 |

* No Games held during World War II

### Women's Competition

| Year | Final Game Score |
|---|---|
| 1976 | Gold, USSR; Silver, United States |
| 1980 | USSR 104, Bulgaria 73 |
| 1984 | United States 85, Korea 55 |
| 1988 | United States 77, Yugoslavia 70 |
| 1992 | Unified Team 76, China 66 |

(Women played a round-robin tournament with the gold medal going to the team with the best record.)

RECORDS

# INDEX

Alcindor, Lew (Kareem Abdul-Jabbar), 16
Amsterdam Games (1928), 12
Atlanta Games (1996), 9, 29
Auerbach, Red, 16

Barcelona Games (1992), 9, 25, 28
Barkley, Charles, 9, 28
basketball
  birth of, 7, 9
  changes in, 13
  first official Olympic game, 12-13
  future of, 28-29
  global improvement, 16
  pro participation, 25, 28, 29
Belov, Aleksandr, 20
Berlin Games (1936), 12-13, 17
Bird, Larry, 9, 28
boycotts, 22
Bradley, Bill, 16
Brazil, 14
bronze medals, 25, 28
Bulgaria, 22

Canada, 13
Carter, Jimmy, 22
Chile, 13
China, 28
Collins, Doug, 20
Cousy, Bob, 16
Croatia, 25, 28
Cuba, 28
Czechoslovakia, 28

Daly, Chuck, 28
demonstration games, 9, 12
Donovan, Anne, 22
Dream Team I, 9, 25-28
Dream Team II, 9, 29

Ewing, Patrick, 22

gold medals, 9, 14, 16, 20, 21, 22, 28

Harris, Lusia, 20
Hayes, Elvin, 16
Haywood, Spencer, 16
Head-Summitt, Pat, 22

Iba, Coach, 17
International Basketball Association, 25
International YMCA Training School, 7, 9
Italy, 22

Jackson, Luke, 16
Johnson, Magic, 9, 28
Jordan, Michael, 9, 22, 28

Knight, Bobby, 22
Korea, 22
Kukoc, Toni, 28

Laettner, Christian, 28
Lieberman, Nancy, 20
Lithuania, 25
London Games (1948), 13
Los Angeles Games (1932), 12
Los Angeles Games (1984), 22
Lucas, Jerry, 14

Manning, Danny, 25
medals. *See* bronze medals; gold medals;
  silver medals
Mexico City Games (1968), 16
Meyers, Ann, 20
Miller, Cheryl, 22
Montreal Games (1976), 20-21
Moscow Games (1980), 21-22
Munich Games (1972), 17

Naismith, James, 7, 13
National Basketball Association (NBA), 28, 29

Paris Games (1924), 12
Philippines, 13-14

Robertson, Alvin, 22
Robertson, Oscar, 14
Robinson, David, 25
Rome Games (1960), 14
Russell, Bill, 13
Russia. *See* Soviet Union

St. Louis Games (1904), 9, 12

cont. next page

# INDEX

Semenova, Iuliyana, 21, 22
Seoul Games (1988), 22
silver medals, 21, 28
Smith, Dean, 20
Soviet Union
 boycott by, 22
 dissolution of, 25
 Olympic losses, 14, 16, 22
 Olympic wins, 17, 20, 25
 women competitors, 20-22, 28
 *see also* Unified Team
Spain, 28
Switzerland, 13

Thailand, 13
Thompson, John, 25
Tokyo Games (1964), 16

Unified Team (former Soviet Union), 28
United States
 boycott by, 22
 Dream Teams, 9, 25-28, 29
 Olympic losses, 17, 25
 Olympic wins, 13-14, 16, 20, 22
 women competitors, 20-22, 28

West, Jerry, 14
White, Jo-Jo, 16
women competitors, 20-22, 28
Wood, Leon, 22
Woodward, Lynette, 22

Yugoslavia (former), 14, 16, 20, 22, 25; *see also* Croatia